MY CUP IS OVERFLOWING

YOUR CUP CAN BE OVERFLOWING TOO!

Devotionals Based On Psalm 23:5

MY CUP IS OVERFLOWING
I'm Drinking From My Saucer

J.J. Turner, Ph.D.

Solutions 2.0, Inc.

Price $12.95 (Subject to change)
To Order:
Solutions 2.0. Inc.
140 Monroe Dr
McDonough, GA 30252
www.jeremiahinstitute.com
Amazon.com

THE 23ʳᵈ PSALM

The Lord is my shepherd
I will always have everything I need.
He lets me lie down in green pastures.
He leads me by calm pools of water.

He gives new strength to my soul
For the good of His name.
He leads me on paths of goodness,
To show he is truly good.

Even if I walk through a valley as dark as the grave,
I will not be afraid of any danger.
Why? Because you are with me, Lord.
Your rod and staff comfort me.

Lord, you prepared my table
In front of my enemies.
You poured oil on my head.
My cup is full and spilling over.

Goodness and mercy will be with me the rest of my
life.
And I will sit in the Lord's temple for a long, long
time.

(Easy-to-Read Version. Pages 584-585)

Now

Is a great Time To

Pray!

DRINKING FROM MY SAUCER*

I have never made a fortune...
And it is probably too late now.
I do not worry about that much
... I am happy anyhow.

For, as I go along the way of life,
I reap better than I have sowed ...
I am drinking from my saucer,
Because my cup has overflowed.

Have not got a lot of riches,
And sometimes the going is tough ...
But there are caring folks around me,
And that makes me rich enough.

I thank God for His blessings,
And the mercies He bestows.
I am drinking from my saucer,
Because my cup has overflowed.

O, remember times when things went wrong,
My faith wore somewhat thin.
But all at once the dark clouds broke,
And the sun peeped through again.

So Lord, help me not to gripe about
The tough rows that I have hoed ...
I am drinking from my saucer,
Because my cup has overflowed.

If God gives me strength and courage
When the going gets steep and rough,
I will not ask for other blessings ...
I am already blessed enough.

And may I never be too busy
To help others bear their loads.
With them I share my saucer,
Because my cup has overflowed.

*NOTE: I have tried to find the author of this song/poem. It has been attributed to such persons as John Paul Moore, Jimmy Dean, and Michale Combs. It has been recorded by numerous artists. If you know the author, please let me know so I may give credit.

MY CUP OVERFLOWS

Because of His amazing grace and love
God has given me a special cup;
It is a spiritual cup
To hold the out-pouring of His blessings.

My cup has an unlimited capacity
Designed by God just for me
To daily receive the benefits
He so graciously fills it with.

It has a no limits capacity
It over-flows every day;
My cup holds the provisions
Given to me by my heavenly Father.

I must not fall into the trap
Of thinking I have no blessings
Or that my cup is smaller
Than the cups of others in Christ.

My cup over-flows every day
And I praise God for this gift;
Asking for wisdom to use the gifts
To praise, honor and serve Him.

(J.J. Turner, Ph.D. © 2014)

I CAN'T PRAY YESTERDAY
IT IS GONE ...
I CAN'T PRAY
TOMORROW...
IT'S NOT HERE YET...
I CAN PRAY NOW...
IT IS HERE!

CONTENT

PREFACE

Stop a person on the street and ask him or her if they have ever heard of the 23rd Psalm, and the answer will usually be yes. Most can even quote part or all of this familiar Psalm. The 23rd Psalm has been called by many the most beautiful affirmation of faith ever written. It is a beacon in the midst of life's storms. It has been used in more funeral services than any other portion of Scripture. Even agnostics and atheist use it. It is amazing!

In six short verses in the English Bible we have a grand declaration by David relative to trusting God, regardless of the circumstances. This Psalm has given courage and comfort to soldiers facing battles, and to persons facing immediate death. Even criminals facing the death penalty find comfort and courage in this Psalm.

The 23rd Psalm has been the subject of more sermons, articles, devotionals, books, and discussions than perhaps any other portion of Scripture. It has an appeal to everyone. Parents sit during the long dark hours of worrying about their children, reading or quoting this Psalm. While holding the hand of a loved one in the hospital the 23rd Psalm runs through the minds of many. *"The Lord is my Shepherd";* five comforting words. Comfort 24-7-365!

This brief book is a reminder to Christians; especially "troubled" Christians how our cup is over flowing with blessing from God. He hasn't brought us this far to let a draught pull blessings from our cup of life; or let a hole trickle them away.

What follows are 26 short devotional reminders of how our cup is overflowing every day; not just on the positive days. There are response areas to help you get the most from the lesson. I encourage you to not only read and enjoy these reminders, but ask you to share them with others. Even younger persons will be encouraged by being re-minded that their cup is overflowing. How has this Psalm blessed your life? How is your cup overflowing?

A BIGGER CUP AND SAUCER

My cup is not just
A fourth, half or near full;
It is overflowing.

God doesn't just give me
Enough to get by;
My cup is spilling over.

Not only is my
Cup overflowing;
My saucer is too.

At first my cup
Was very small and shallow,
But God gave me a
Bigger and deeper one:
Even now it is overflowing.

No matter what I need
I have more than enough:
My cup is overflowing
From God's bounty.

God isn't stingy
With His blessings;
He daily fills my
Cup to an overflowing.

God not only
Gives me the cup;
He fills it

To an overflowing wonder.

I don't have to wait
Until heaven;
I am blessed now:
My cup is running over.

My cup is filled
With everlasting water;
It is never empty;
My cup is overflowing.

I am not promised
A trickle of water,
But a river of water
That overflows my cup.

My cup and saucer
Are always overflowing,
And God keeps on
Pouring out His blessings.

Good keeps on giving me
A bigger cup
And a bigger saucer;
But they keep overflowing too.

(J.J. Turner © 2014)

INTRODUCTION

Imagine how you would feel if your son was chasing you and trying to kill you. This, according to the preponderance of scholarship, is the one of two or three possible backgrounds to the 23rd Psalm. Absalom, David's son, was trying to kill him.

Absalom, in our today's language, tried to create a coo to overthrow His father David's reign as king. In 2 Samuel 15 we read the account of Absalom's tactics of gaining favor with the people. All his efforts were designed to undermine the credibility of His father, David. He succeeded.

Finally Absalom's tactics worked. In 2 Samuel 15:13-24 we read the account of David fleeing from his son, Absalom: *"Now a messenger came to David, saying, 'The heart of the men of Israel are with Absalom.' So David said to all his servants who were with him at Jerusalem, 'Arise, and let us flee, or we shall not escape from Absalom. Make haste to depart, lest he overtake us suddenly and bring disaster upon us, and we strike the city with the edge of the sword.' And the king's servants said to the king, 'We are your servants, ready to do whatever my lord the king commands."* And the king went out with all his household after him. But the king left ten women, concubines, to keep the house. And the king went out with all the people after him, and stopped at the outskirts. Then all his servants passed before him; and all the Cherethites, and the Pelethites, and all the Gittites, six hundred men who followed him from Gath, passed before the king."

Prior to the move by Absalom to kill David, king Saul had tried to do the same thing. This story is recorded in 1 Samuel 23-24. So whether the background of the 23rd Psalm is the events with Absalom or with king Saul, or even during the numerous wars David engaged in, he knew that the LORD WAS HIS SHEPHERD." God was his sustainer!

The message transcends to us today. Regardless of the circumstances in life, the *Lord is our Shepherd and our cup overflows!*

FOR THOUGHT AND DISCUSSION

1. Can you recall a time n your life when God sustained you?

2. How does the 23rd Psalm comfort you?

3. How do you share the 23rd Psalm with others?

CLOSER LOOK AT THE 23rd PSALM

Years ago I heard a sermon on the 23rd Psalm in which the speaker presented a grammatical look at the key words in the first verse of the 23rd Psalm. I want to share them as part of our introduction to our study:

(1) **THE**—there is no doubt that the Lord is the only Shepherd. The definitive article adds to the truth of the statement in the Psalm. This is also an affirmation of a relationship with the true Shepherd. We are not strangers.

(2) **LORD**—this affirms that there is only one Lord; He is the creator, owner and ruler over all. Jesus is our Lord (cf. Luke 6:46), not some man or council of men.

(3) **IS**—this acknowledged that the Lord is not going to be his shepherd in the future but He is presently his shepherd. He is trusted and relied on now.

(4) **MY**—he didn't say "our Shepherd" which would have been true, he said *"my Shepherd"*. He is making it personal. This means to me that I can make this statement personal, too.

(5) **SHEPHERD**—this is a dynamic recognition of the fact that God is the one true Shepherd. He can be trusted for guidance, safety, feeding, and other blessings only a true shepherd can give. Jesus is our Shepherd today; we can trust Him (cf. John chapter 10).

(6) **I**—again the promise is taken very personally. It belong to ME, as if I were the only person alive who needs to be protected by the Shepherd.

(7) **SHALL**—this is a recognition that the Shepherd's protection wasn't something in the past, but is now and in the future. It doesn't expire.

(8) **NOT**—this means that I will never have a need that the Shepherd will not take care of; His protection is always with me.

(9) **WANT**—this is not a blank check that I can ask the Lord for anything I want; it means that within the realm of my spiritual needs, He will meet them.

This verse sets the stage for what follows. What follows will be true because of these nine truths. It is because of these truths that our CUP OVERFLOWS.

It is now time to look at some of our over-flowing blessings. Is you cup and saucer ready to be filled and overflowing?

THE CATALYST FOR MY OVERFLOWING CUP

Catalysis: (n) _"A person or thing acting as a stimulus in bringing about or hastening a result."_

There is one catalysis, and one catalyst only, for causing my cup to overflow. The catalysis is my heavenly Father. The giver of perfect gifts.

There are numerous passages of Scripture that affirm my special relationship with God, my heavenly Father. It is out of this relationship that my cup overflows. This is very exciting!

Here are a few of those Scriptures and reasons I know God is the catalyst for my overflowing cup:

1. **I am created in the image of God:** _"So God created man in His own image; in the image of God He created him; male and female He created them"_ (Genesis 1:27).

2. **I am the apple of God's eye:** _"Keep me as the apple of Your eye; hide me under the shadow of Your wings"_ Psalm 17:8).

3. **God holds me by my right hand:** *"Nevertheless I am continually with You; You hold me by my right hand"* *Psalm 73:23).*

4. **God is my strength:** *"The Lord God is my strength; He will make my feet like deer's feet, and He will make me walk on my high hills" (Habakkuk 3:19).*

5. **God gives only good and perfect gifts:** *"Every good gift and every perfect gift is from above, and comes down from the Father of lights, with whom there is no variation or shadow or turning" (James 1:17).*

How encouraging to know that the overflowing of my spiritual blessing cup doesn't depends on things or men, but upon God. He is the catalyst.

What are some additional reminders of why God is the catalyst for our overflowing cups?

1)._____

2)._____

3)._____

CUP DRAINERS

Not long ago I bought a donut and a cup of coffee. I set my coffee in the cup holder in the middle console of my car, as I wolfed down the donut. When I reached for my coffee, I noticed a puddle of coffee around it in the holder which allowed the coffee to drain out. There was a leak in the cup.

While we are given the promise that our Shepherd will cause our cup to continually over-flow with blessings and protection, we must be alert to the fact that there are potential cup drainers that we must guard against.

Here are a few of the cup drainers we must be on guard against:

First, as you might guess, Satan is the leaders of the cup draining brigade. Peter warns us of this truth: *"Be sober, be vigilant; because your adversary the devil walks about like a roaring lion, seeking whom he may devour" (1 Peter 5:8).* As Christians, one way he tries to drain our cup is trying to convince us that we are too old to be of any use to the Lord and His church. Can you think of other ways the Devil seeks to drain our cup? "The youth are too young."

Second, fear is a major drainer of our blessing cup. As we grow older we fear aging, health problems, financial issues, and ultimately death. This is contrary to what God has placed in our cup of blessings. Paul wrote: *"For God has not given us a spirit of fear, but of power and of love and of a sound mind" (2 Timothy 1:7).* Remember that fear has been defined as:

False
Evidence
Appearing
Real

Third, our blessing cup is drained by our choice of attitude. One of the major criticisms of older people is their negative and critical attitudes toward life and people. It's the "I don't care what song you play, as long as you play something sad and blue." As Christians, young or old, we are commanded to have the "attitude of Christ" (Philippians 2:4-9). This means to be free from pessimism, worry, criticism, anger, arrogance, and such like. God has given us a thinking agenda in Philippians 4:6-10.

Fourth, a lack of faith is a major drainer of our blessing cup. We may think we have a lot of things going for us as faithful Christians, but if we don't have faith, we aren't pleasing God. *"But without faith it is impossible to please ,* *for he who comes to God must believe that He is, and that He is a rewarder of those who diligently seek Him"* (Hebrews 11:6).

Fifth, a lack of knowledge drains our cup. In the Old Testament, Hosea declared, speaking for God, *"My people are destroyed for a lack of knowledge"* (Hoses 4:6-8). Truth, according to Jesus, is the only things that will set us free (John 8:32). Jesus is that truth (John 8:36; 14:6). We must not only know the truth but practice it also (cf. James 1:22-26). A lack of knowing and doing the truth is a bag of termites that eat a hole in our cup of blessings. Ignorance drains us.

We must be continually on guard relative to possible drainers of our blessing cup. What are some possible additional drainers of our blessing cup? List some:

1)._____

_____

_____

_____

2)._____

_____

_____

_____

MY OVERFLOWING CUP

Imagine with me a very hot summer day. Thirst is attacking your entire being. Your mouth and throat are dry; you feel a little dizzy. Your lips are starting to feel parched. Finally you make it to a local diner and quickly order a glass of water. You guzzle it too fast but you are thirsty beyond words. The glass is empty in seconds but almost instantly it is refilled, as if by magic or a miracle. In fact it starts to overflow with cool water, and you drink and drink.

While this may be a myth for illustration purposes; it is a simple metaphor of how God continually fills and refills our cup with blessings. No matter how much is removed or depleted it seems, it never empties; it continues not only full but overflows. Its God way of saying, "I love you" (John 3:16).

The appetite that keeps our cup over-flowing is, in the words of Jesus, *"Blessed are those who hunger and thirst for righteousness, for they shall be filled" (Matthew 5:6).* Cups that aren't thirsty aren't filled or over-flowing. How thirsty are you?

The thirst that guarantees the over-flowing of blessings is described by the Psalmist in 42:1, 2, *"As a deer pants for water brooks, so pants my soul for you O God. My soul thirst for God, for the living God. When shall I come to appear before God?"*

Jesus reminded us of the *"cup of the new covenant" (Mark 12:22-26).* Paul wrote, *"The cup of the blessing which we bless, is it not the communion of the blood of Christ. The bread which we break, is it not the communion of the body of Christ?" (1 Corinthians 10:16).*

My over-flowing cup of blessing is guaranteed by the cup of Christ's shed blood. It is continually a reality in my life as *"I walk in the light as He is in the light" (1 John 1:7).* His blood continually cleanses me.

How do you intentionally maintain an awareness of your relationship to the "cup of Christ's blood" and your over-flowing cup of blessings? State some ways:

1)._____

_____

_____

_____

2)._____

_____

_____

_____

3)._____

_____

_____

MY CUP OVERFLOWS WITH FORGIVENESS

"I'll forgive you but I don't want to."

"You'll have to earn my forgiveness."

"I'll never forgive you."

These, sadly, are frequent remarks we hear, even from Christians, about forgiving someone. I am thankful to my heavenly Father that He doesn't have these attitudes. Why? Because I stand in need of forgiveness 24-7-365. I'm sure you do too.

At the top of my list of identified overflowings from my cup is FORGIVENESS. What if our Father only granted forgiveness 70x7=490 times, as we are commanded to do (cf. Matthew 18:21, 22). Well, I would have run out of forgivenesses by Him a long time ago; and not being judgmental, but you would have too. Why? We all sin continually (cf. 1 John 1:5-9; Romans 3:23).

Talk about forgiveness! How about this reference by the Psalmist? *"As far as the east is from the west,*
So far has He REMOVED our transgressions from us" (Psalm 103:12). Jeremiah adds this promise of forgiveness under the new covenant: *"... For I will forgive their iniquity, and*

their sin I will remember no more" (Jeremiah 31:34). Now this is Good News!

My cup overflows with forgiveness continually as I *"walk in the light as He is in the light"(1 John 1:7).* God has made provisions for our forgiveness: *"If we confess our sins. He is faithful and just to forgive us our sins and to cleanse us from all unrighteousness" (1 John 1:9).*

Does God have a limit relative to the kinds of sins he forgives? No, not according to 1 Corinthians 6:9-11. The blood of Christ is sufficient for the removal of all sins (cf. Matthew 26:28). Yes, even that one!

How has the blessing of having all your sins forgiven impacted your life?:

1)._____

_____

_____

_____

MY CUP OVERFLOWS WITH JOY

As they were driving along one day after church, little eight-year-old Tommy asked his father, "Dad, are mules Christians?"

In a state of surprised the father replied, "Son, what made you ask that? That isn't nice."

"Well," Tommy replied, "they have long faces too."

We've all heard "What you are speaks so loudly, I can't hear what you are saying." Many Christians, who should have cups over-flowing with joy, have just the opposite as they sing "troublesome times are here." Their motto seems to be "I don't' care what you play as long as you play something blue."

One of my favorite children's songs says, "I've got the joy, joy, joy down in my heart. Where? Down in my heart." I think we need to sing this song frequently in our assemblies.

Every day should be a day of joy and rejoicing for God's children. Joy should be allowed to over-flow our cup. The Psalmist reminds us that joy should be a daily expression,

"This is the day the Lord has made; we will rejoice and be glad in it" (Psalm 118:24).

An old grouch, upon hearing this verse quoted, asked sarcastically, "What is there to rejoice and be glad about? Life stinks." A friend replied, "Just try missing one of these days and you'll know."

We need to read Paul's epistle to the Philippians in order to see the full blessings of joyfulness. We have everything from the joy of salvation to the joy of heaven. Paul affirmed that even praying for them was a joy (Philippians 1:4). Is your cup overflowing with joy? It's a personal choice only you can make.

List five things you have to be joyful about:

1)._____

_____

_____

2)._____

_____

_____

3)._____

_____

_____

4)._____

_____

_____

5)._____

_____

_____

MY CUP OVERFLOWS WITH LOVE

Love! Few words in the English language are tossed about more than **love**; yet, it is also very misunderstood and abused by many. People express their love for everything from their car to their dog; from their jobs to their houses; from clothing to family, etc. Seems like everything is loved.

As Christians our cup over-flows with God's love. We have heard and quoted John 3:16 so many times that it's like the proverbial "water on a duck's back": it moves away so quickly. Here is that beautiful and inspiring verse again for us to read and meditate on: *"For God so loved the world that He gave His only begotten Son, that whoever believes in Him should not perish but have everlasting life" (John 3:16).*

Regardless of what we have or have not done, God, Who created us in His image, loves us—not our sin, but us. His gift of eternal life is offered to all.

It is in the death of Christ on the cross that I fully see and realize how much God loves me, and how my cup is overflowing with His love. *"For when we were still without strength, in due time Christ died for the ungodly. For* scarcely for a righteous man will one die; yet, perhaps for a good man someone would even dare to die. But God demonstrated his own love toward us, in that while we were still sinners, Christ died for us" (Romans 5:6-8).

Not only is my cup over-flowing with love from God, it is also over-flowing with love from my brethren. Here is Jesus' command: "A new commandment I give to you, that you love one another; as I have loved you, that you also love one another. By this all will know that you are My disciples, if you have love for one another" (John 13:34, 35).

In his letter to the Corinthians, chapter 13, the apostle Paul gave a list of behaviors and attitudes that express the kind of love (i.e. agape) God wants us to have for each other in the Body of Christ. These are ways to share our overflowing cup of love.

How are some ways you can intentionally demonstrate your overflowing love to others?:

1)._____

_____

_____

_____

2)._____

_____

_____

3)_____

_____

_____

MY CUP OVERFLOWS WITH FAITH

We can have a lot of positive things going for us, such as charm, knowledge of languages, wealth, positions, speaking ability, and so forth, but *"without faith it is IMPOSSIBLE to please God" (Hebrews 11:6)*. What a clear word: Impossible.

In the midst of inquiring for an answer to "What is faith?" God's word gives us the answer. Faith is the flood gate that opens an over-flowing of my spiritual cup. Here's how the Hebrews writer defined it: *"Now faith is the substance of things hoped for, the evidence of things not seen. For by it the elders obtained a good testimony" (Hebrews 11:1, 2)*. The rest of the eleventh chapter is a list of faithful people; people who are in heaven cheering us on: *"Great cloud of witnesses"* (cf. Hebrews chapter 12).

It is not the amount of my faith, but the quality of my faith that pleases God and causes my cup to over-flow. Jesus said if I have faith *"as large as a mustard seed"*, I could move mountains.

On my spiritual journey, when I get to those "Red Sea" places in my life, which come frequently, I just trust Him by placing my toes in the water and walking on across my problem. "Faith is the victory! I just "hold to God's unchanging hand."

To say my cup overflows with faith is not bragging, but a simple statement of my trust in God. It is the intent of my heart to serve Him moment by moment, day by day, for as long as I journey here below (cf. Hebrews 4:12). I will die faithfully (Revelation 2:10).

Here is my simple acrostic of F-A-I-T-H:

F-ollowing Christ (where He leads me, Matthew 16:24))
A-ttitude of Christ (having His attitude, Philippians 2:4-9)
I-n His light (I am walking; 1 John 1:7)
T-rusting God (no matter what happens; Job 13:15)
H-eaven awaits (Revelation 2:10).

What are some intentional ways you demonstrate your faith?:

1)._____

_____

_____

_____

2)._____

_____

_____

_____

3)._____

_____

_____

_____

MY CUP OVERFLOWS WITH PURPOSE

What if you were asked, "What have you done as a major purpose in your life that you believe in and are proud about achieving?" It might amaze you to hear that many people can't identify a unique purpose that creates excitement in their lives. Thoreau, the literary genius, said, "Most men live lives of quiet desperation." Surely, not Christians!

Dostoyevsky wrote, "The mystery of human existence lies not in just staying alive, but in finding something to live for." The apostle Paul affirmed his purpose in life, *"For me to live is Christ, to die is gain."* How is that for a cup overflowing with purpose? The saucer is filled too!

H.G. wells, famous philosopher and historian, said at the age of 61, "I have no peace. All life is at the end of the tether." The famous poet, Lord Byron said, "My days are in yellow leaf, the flowers and fruit of life are gone, the worm and the canker, and the grief are mine alone."

George Bernard Shaw, wrote: "This is the true joy in life, the being used for a purpose by yourself as a mighty one: the being thoroughly worn out before you are thrown on the scrap heap, and being a force of nature instead of a feverish selfish little clod of ailments and grievances, complaining that the world will not devote itself to making you happy."

As Christians our cups overflow with major purposes. Here are a few of them:

1. **My daily purpose is to glorify God:** *"To Him be glory in the church by Christ Jesus to all generations, forever and ever. Amen" (Ephesians 3:21).* There can be no higher purpose than this. To get up every day with the blessing of bringing God glory (cf. Revelation 4:11).

2. **My daily purpose is to imitate God:** *"Therefore be imitators of God as dear children" (Ephesians 5:1).* People tend to imitate persons they admire. No privilege could be greater than being allowed to imitate God, our heavenly Father.

3. **My daily purpose is to keep the unity of the Spirit:** *"I therefore, the prisoner of the Lord, beseech you to walk worthy of your calling with which you were called, with all lowliness and gentleness, with long*

suffering, bearing with one another in love, endeav-
oring to keep the unity of the Spirit in the bond of
peace" (Ephesians 4:1-3).

There is no doubt, based on Scriptures, that as Christians, our cup overflows. We should let our feet hit the floor every day with a song in our hearts and a snap in our step. "Got a good reason for living."

Name three additional major purposes we have as Christians:

1)._____

_____

_____

2)._____

_____

_____

3)._____

_____

_____

MY CUP OVERFLOWS WITH ASSURANCE

Sadly, I once heard about a group of preachers who were asked, "Are you sure you are saved?" Out of the seventeen, only six were very sure; five thought if everything worked out right at the end of their lives, they'd be saved; and the rest thought it would be arrogant to say yes. Some thought it was a "denominational display of arrogance and false doctrine", to say you are saved.

Many Christians share the belief and attitudes of these preachers. Some seem to believe that God is keeping a record book in which He documents our pluses and minuses; and if we die not having "prayed up, attended enough, and given enough," we may be in danger of missing heaven. If we slip on a banana peeling and happen to say the wrong words, and die, we will miss heaven. How sad!

My cup over-flows with the assurance of salvation. No! This is no arrogance but Bible truth. First, the apostle John wrote that we can know we are saved: *"These things I have written to you who believe in the name of the Son of God, that you may KNOW THAT YOU HAVE ETERNAL LIFE, and that you may continue to believe in the name of the Son of God" (1 John 5:13).*

After dealing with the frustrations and his inability to keep the law in Romans chapter 7, the apostle Paul affirmed the assurance of his salvation in Christ: *"There is therefore now NO CONDEMNATION to those who are in Christ Jesus, who do not walk according to the flesh, but according to the Spirit" (Romans 8:1).*

My assurance of salvation in Christ is also guaranteed as a results of walking properly. *"But if we walk in the light as He is in the light, we have fellowship with one another, and the blood of Jesus Christ His Son cleanses us from ALL sin" (1 John 1:7).* The phrase *"cleanses us"* is perpetual in the Greek, and means *"It keeps on cleansing us."*

Like Paul, *"I know in Whom I have believed, and am persuaded that He is able to keep that which I have committed to His trust until that day."*

What are some additional reasons we can know we are saved?:

1)._____

_____

_____

2)._____

_____

_____

3)._____

_____

_____

MY CUP OVERFLOWS WITH RESOURCES

Have you ever had a job or assignment but didn't have the resources to complete either one? I have, and it was very frustrating. However, when it comes to the Christian life, this isn't the case. We have all the resources we need to be and do what God wants us to do and be.

Sadly, some seem to think Christianity is a religion that is basically a do-it-yourself proposition. One old timer said, "God gave me a King James Bible, placed me in a canoe and told me to paddle my way to the pearly gates." This is an affront to God's love and grace.

The Psalmist wrote this about the resources that God has placed at our disposal: *"Bless the Lord, O my soul, and forget not all his benefits: Who forgives all your iniquities, Who heals all your diseases, Who redeems your life from destruction, Who crowns you with loving-kindness and tender mercies, Who satisfies your mouth with good things, so that your youth is renewed like the eagle's" (Psalm 103:1-5).*

My cup overflows with spiritual resources. Here are a few of these resources:

✓ **Prayer** is a major resource God has blessed me with. James reminds us of this blessing: *If any of you lack wisdom, let him ask God, who gives to all liberally and without reproach, and it will be given him"...* *"fervent prayer of a righteous man avails much"* *(James 1:4; 5:16).* Don't stop praying; the answer is coming!

✓ **Power** is a major resource God has blessed me with: *"Now to Him who is able to do exceedingly abundantly above all that we ask or think, according to the power that works in us" (Ephesians 3:20).* It is on the basis of this power that *"I can do all things in Christ."*

✓ **Blessings** are a major resource in Christ. *"Blessed be the God and Father of our Lord Jesus Christ, who has blessed us with EVERY spiritual blessing in the heavenly places in Christ" (Ephesians 1:3).* We need to daily sing, "Count your blessings, and name them one by one, and it will surprise you what the Lord has done."

List some additional resources you have in Christ that are overflowing:

1)._____

2)._____

3)._____

4)._____

MY CUP OVERFLOWS WITH TRUST

Have you noticed how life is based on trust? In every direction, there are evidences of trust. We take our car to a mechanic, trusting that he will not cheat us. We undergo the scalpel of an unknown surgeon, trusting our lives to his hands. We enter our credit card number on a computer, trusting it will not be hacked. We drive down the highway, trusting that the oncoming driver will stay on his side of the road. Life is one trust event after another.

The persons who utters, "I don't trust anyone", isn't telling the whole truth. When he picks up a can or package of food in the grocery store, he is thereby trusting that it is not laced with poison. When he places a letter in the mail slot, he is trusting that the mailman will not destroy it. Try as we may, or deny as loudly as we can, trust is an escapable part of everyday life. We can't avoid it.

I have a spiritual cup that overflows with trust. This trust is in the Father, Son, and Holy Spirit: The Godhead. Solomon wrote: *Trust in the LORD with all your heart and lean not on your understanding" (Proverbs 3:5)*. He also tells us that *"He who trusts in himself is a fool..." (Proverbs 28:26)*.

It is relatively easy to trust God when the sun is shining and all is going well. But when the storms come, and life caves in; it becomes more difficult to trust God. This wasn't how Job, the ancient suffering man of God felt after he had lost everything except his wife. On the dung heap he said, *"Though He slay me, yet will I trust Him."* Now that's a cup overflowing with trust in God!

David said that when he walked through the valley of the shadow of death, he would trust God. On the cross, Jesus trusted His Father, *"Into your hands I commit my spirit."* King David said, *"Do not be afraid or discouraged, for the LORD God, my God, is with you. He will not fail you or forsake you ..." (1 Chronicles 28:20).*

List some reasons why your trust cup is overflowing:

1)._____

_____

_____

2)._____

_____

_____

3)._____

_____

_____

MY CUP OVERFLOWS WITH GRACE

Few hymns are more popular than John Newton's *Amazing Grace*. This song, which happens to be my favorite hymn, is sung and played at events ranging from ball games to funerals; from church worship services to country music stations: *"Amazing grace, how sweet the sound, that saved a wretch like me,"* is affirmation in song relative to how my cup is overflowing with God's amazing grace.

To the church in Ephesus that had members who *"were once dead in the sins and trespasses and sins" (Ephesians 2:1);* the apostle Paul reminds them of the cause of their salvation. It is God's grace: *"For by grace you have been saved through faith, and that not of yourselves; it is the gift of God, not of works, lest anyone should boast" (Ephesians 2:8, 9).*

Contrary to the thinking of some, God's grace isn't a line drawn in the spiritual sand; a line if you pass over, all hope is lost. To a group of Christians who were fighting and quarreling with each other, behavior contrary to God's grace, James wrote about the extension of God's grace: *"But He gives MORE grace. Therefore He says: 'God resists the proud, but gives MORE grace to the humble.' Therefore submit to God. Resist the Devil and he will flee from you"* (James 4:6, 7).

Some seem to think God is like a stern father, who when ask for money, replies with, "How much do you need to get by?" The thinking is that God gives us enough for "initial salvation", but that's where the line is drawn. We must stay within the confines of the initial gift of grace. James denies this. God gives more grace. Yes, even to you and me!

Since God gives more grace, some of the Christians in Rome evidently thought that since God gives more grace when we sin, therefore, let's sin so we will receive more grace. To this attitude, Paul said no (Romans 6:1-3).

What are some of your responses to the amazing truth that God gives more grace?:

1)._____

_____

_____

2)._____

_____ _____

_____

3)._____

_____

_____

MY CUP OVERFLOWS WITH BOLDNESS

Scared and hiding behind closed doors. This should not be the behavior of a group of men who had been trained to be world-changers. Yet this is where we find the Apostles chosen by Christ. After His illegal arrest, illegal trail, and death on a cross, they were scared; afraid that perhaps they would be next.

Here is John's account of this event: *Then, the same day at evening, being the first day of the week, when the doors were shut where the disciples were assembled, for FEAR of the Jews, Jesus came and stood in the midst, and said to them, 'Peace be with you'"* (John 20:19).

Isn't it amazing what can happens when Jesus shows up? These men go from being coward to courageous; from fear to faith. From cups almost drained to cups overflowing.

As we travel to the Day of Pentecost and the establishment of the church; the coming of the Holy Spirit, and 3000 converts in one day, we thereafter see a totally new group of men. They become men who are sold on being bold. Their spiritual cups are overflowing with boldness. This is seen throughout the book of Acts.

It's amazing how things changed after the Master showed up in their midst. The Apostles would never be found hiding behind closed doors or hiding in any other place. They now had cups that were overflowing with boldness. *"Now when they saw the boldness of Peter and John, and perceived that they were uneducated and untrained men, they marveled. And realized that they had been with Jesus" (Acts 4:13).*

One of the keys to their cups overflowing with boldness was their prayers for boldness: *"Now, Lord, look on their threats, and grant to Your servants that with all boldness they may speak Your word... And when they had prayed, the place where they were assembled together was shaken; and they were all filled with the Holy Spirit, and they spoke the word of God with boldness" (Acts 4:29, 31).*

1). How often do you pray for boldness?

_____

2). What's the boldest thing you've done for the Lord?_____

_____

3). When was the last time you heard prayers in an assembly for boldness?_____

4). How can you increase your boldness?_____

_____

MY CUP OVERFLOWS WITH FELLOWSHIP

The Psalmist reminds us of how wonderful it is to be in fellowship with our brethren. It is one of the blessings that overflows our cup:

"Behold, how good and how pleasant it is
For brethren to dwell together in unity!
It is like the precious oil upon the head
Running down on the beard of Aaron,
Running down on the edge of his garments.
It is like the dew of Hermon,
Descending upon the mountains of Zion;
For there the Lord commanded
The blessing—life forevermore"

(Psalm 133).

The prophet Isaiah saw a time when people from all nations would flow into the house of God (Isaiah 2:2-4). They would cease hostility toward one another; they would become mutual seekers after peace. The Gospel would call all people to be reconciled into one body, the church, to God through Christ (Romans 1:14-16). God's united nation.

This fellowship is demonstrated in our love for one another in the church, and is noted by all who observe it (John 13:34, 35).

This fellowship is maintained with one another, as well as with God, as we walk in the light: *"But if we walk in the light as He is in the light, we have fellowship with one another, and the blood of Jesus Christ His Son cleanses us from all sin" (1 John 1:7).*

In 1 Corinthians 12, the apostle Paul uses the human anatomy to instruct us relative to the uniqueness of our relationship in the body of Christ. For example in verses 26 and 27 he writes, *"And if one member suffers, all the members suffer with it; or if one member is honored, and the members rejoice with it. Now you are the body of Christ, and members individually....".* WE are ONE in Christ.

Because of this overflowing fellowship with my brethren, I do not want to miss any of the assemblies of the church (cf. Hebrews 10:24, 25).

1). How involved are you in the fellowship of the church?_____

_____

2). What are some ways we can improve our fellowship in the church?_____

MY CUP OVERFLOWS WITH ZEAL

"A person who has a rusty wrench and uses it with enthusiasm, will accomplish ten times as much as a lazy person with a tool box filled with all the latest tools." Solomon struck a blow against the lazy or hap-hazard approach to achievement. *"Whatever your hand finds to do, do it with your might; for there is no work or device or knowledge or wisdom in the grave where you are going" (Ecclesiastes 9:10).*

In his epistle to Titus, the apostle Paul encouraged him to be zealous in the Lord's work. *"[W]ho gave Himself for us, that He might redeem us from every lawless deed and purify for Himself His own special people, zealous for good works" (Titus 2:14).*

There are so many things that cause my cup to over-flow with zeal; the least of which is my salvation and all spiritual blessings in Christ. I am a child of God and joint heir with Christ. Through Christ I can do all things; and am more than a conqueror. I've read the end of the story and I win.

In the midst of my rejoicing over the reasons for my cup overflowing with zeal, I must remember that I can become lukewarm. This is what Jesus taught in His remarks to the church of the Laodiceans: *"I know your works that you are neither cold nor hot, I could wish you were cold or hot. So then, because you are lukewarm, and neither cold nor hot, I will vomit you out of my mouth" (Revelation 3:15, 16).*

The word ZEAL (zesto) in the Greek language mean to be "white hot." It is a picture of a piece of steel being places in an inferno and becoming white with heat. God wants us to be "white with heat" for Him and His work. It's the attitude of Jeremiah when he said, *"But his word was in my heart like a burning fire. Shut up in my bones; I was weary of holding it back, and could not" (Jeremiah 20:9).*

Here's how I demonstrate my zeal for God and His work in my behavior:

1)._____

_____

_____

2)._____

_____

_____

MY CUP OVERFLOWS WITH HOPE

Hope! A six-year-old says, "I hope I get a train for my birthday." A traveler thinks, "I hope the plane is on time." Our lives are filled with expressions of hope. I think hope is like love in many respects—over used and misunderstood.

Biblically speaking HOPE is not like a child hoping for a train, or I hope the plane is on time. Hope is not a wish or dream of something that is in doubt of happening. From time to time I hear Christians say, "I hope I am saved and will go to heaven."

As a child of God, I have a cup that over-flows with hope. Here's Paul's words: *"For we were saved by hope, but hope that is seen is not hope; for why does one still hope for what he sees? But if we hope for what we do not see, we eagerly wait for it with perseverance" (Romans 8:24, 25).*

Biblical faith is "desire plus expectation." For example, I desire to go to heaven, and I am expecting to go to heaven based on the atoning work of Christ (cf. Matthew 26:29). Thus, I know I have salvation (cf. 1 John 5:13). Hope is part of the abiding trilogy promised by God: *"And now abide faith, hope, and love, these three; but the greatest of these is love"* (1 Corinthians 13:13).

My cup overflows with hope because it is grounded in the truth of the Gospel (Romans 1:14-16). It is not arrogance to expect what God has promised; it is one of the facets of faith. As the hymn says, "My hope is built on nothing less that Jesus' blood and righteousness."

Think about the promises of God. I am expecting *"all spiritual blessing in Christ"* (Ephesians 1:3-7). I am expecting a home that is prepare and reserved for me in heaven (cf. John 14:6; 1 Peter 1:1-7). I am expecting my sins to be continually washed away as I walk in the light (1 John 1:7). These, and more, are reasons my cup over flows with hope.

Why is hope misunderstood by some people?_____

_____

_____

_____

What are some additional things you have hope of or in?:

1)._____

_____

2)._____

_____

MY CUP OVERFLOWS WITH WONDER

Today I was taking a walk by the lake in my community. The water was like a glass mirror; ducks were swimming; even saw a fish jump out of the water to see if the sun had come up. Birds were singing; the buzzards were about their work of cleaning up the squirrels that had been hit by cars while crossing the road. For a small moment in time I was really seeing the wonders of God's creation. I am around this every day, but I don't SEE it. Why?

My cup overflows with the wonders of God's creations, as well as so many things created by the hands of men, such as music, art, and literature. In the context of commanding His followers not to worry, Jesus gave the therapy of observing God's wonders (cf. Matthew 6:25-33). When we see how God sustains the world, we can trust Him to sustain us.

In Psalm 139, the Psalmist penned some amazing words about the wonder of our being: *"I will praise You, for I am fearfully and wonderfully made; marvelous are Your works, and that my soul knows very well" (Psalm 139:14).*

From time to time I stop to gaze into our church nursery. What a joy and blessing to see the wonder of children. To see their smiles, hear their crying; realizing they are God's gift; the future of the church. Living and breathing wonders. It's amazing.

If we will but be still, open our eyes and ears, we will be bathed with the overflowing of wonders in God's universes. Yet, an even greater wonder is that in spite of the vastness of the universes, God is mindful of me. This is what the Psalmist declared in 139:7-17. Jesus even said God has assigned a number to each hair on our head; He is even aware of the death of a sparrow. Wow! How awesome! I am actually a wonder, too.

I once thought I would like to travel and see the **Seven Wonders** of the ancient world. I would still like to do so, but I know it will not happen. I realize every day, more and more, that I live in a world of present and ancient wonders: The works of God's hands. I need to enjoy the overflowing of these in my life and spiritual cup. *"He has made everything beautiful in its own time" (King Solomon).*

What are some possible reasons we usually miss the present wonders all around us?:

1)._____

_____

2)._____

_____

3)._____

_____

How will you intentionally benefit from the wonders around you?:_____

_____

_____

_____

MY CUP OVERFLOWS WITH GRATITUDE

In the Sunday morning sermon the preacher had said that every day was thanksgiving. On the way home, little Johnny asked his parents, *Well, if every day is thanksgiving, why don't we have turkey for dinner every day?* Kids ask amazing questions!

We smile at little Johnny's question because we know that every day should be a day of gratitude and thankfulness; even though we don't have turkey but once a year to celebrate the holiday.

A survey among waiters and waitresses revealed that about half of all customers say "thank you" when being served. More and more we hear parents coaxing children to say thank you. We are becoming more and more a nation of thankless people; a nation where entitlement is expected, not something to be thankful for. We live in a ME generation!

A failure to be thankful, according to the Bible, is a sin, a behavior that displeases God. Paul said it is one of the reasons God gave up the Gentile: *[B]ecause, although they knew God, they did not glorify Him as God, nor were thankful, but became futile in their thoughts, and their foolish minds were darkened" (Romans 1:21).*

Among all the people who should be thankful, the Christian has a cup that should be overflowing with gratitude. Have you ever tried, as the song suggests, to count your blessing, naming them one by one? It is impossible. Go ahead and try it!

In your opinion why is there a lack of gratitude today?:

1)._____

_____

2)._____

_____

How can we promote gratitude?:

1)._____

2)._____

3)._____

MY CUP OVERFLOWS WITH OPTIMISM

Two men look though prison bars, one sees mud, the other sees stars. We live in a world where when a person is asked, what kind of music do you want to hear? They reply, I don't care what you play as long as you play something blue. And sadly for many Christians their favorite song is, "Troublesome times are here."

It has been said that if we hear something negative we will tell eleven persons; if we hear something positive or good, we will tell three persons. Good news travels fast, but bad news travels at lightening speed.

As an optimistic child of God, I don't see the cup as either half-full or half-empty. I see it overflowing with God's blessings. I choose to believe and apply the words of Browning: "The best is yet to be." And the words of Paul, "I am more than a conqueror in Christ." The Godhead is "working all things for my good (cf. Romans 8:25-29). "Greater is He Who is in me, than he who is in the world." "I can do all things through Christ." I've read the end of the story: WE WIN! I have much to be optimistic about.

Pessimism is contrary to the attitude of Christ. We are commanded to have His attitude (cf. Philippians 2:4-9). My attitude is the result of my thinking (cf. Proverbs 23:7; Mark 7:21-25). God has given me a thinking agenda to help me be optimistic (Philippians 4:8-10). The choice is mine.

I need to work on the attitude that, regardless of my trials, I will "count them as all joy" (cf. James 1:1-4). This is the true test of optimism.

What are some additional reasons our cups overflow with optimism?:

1)._____

2)._____

3)._____

MY CUP OVERFLOWS WITH POWER

An aged Christian who was confined to a wheelchair, was being questioned about his handicap. His reply was inspiring. He said, "Don't let my age and being in this wheelchair fool you. I am a son of God and join heir with Jesus Christ. And I have an unbelievable power at my disposal."

It almost seems like a contradiction; the fact that we are "cheap clay pots" (2 Corinthians 4:7), but at the same time we have an amazing resource of power that is ours.

While my flesh and mental capacity may not be the strongest, my spiritual power is TNT. Here's is what Paul wrote about the presence of power in his life: *"Therefore do not be ashamed of the testimony of our Lord, nor of His prisoner, but share with me in the sufferings for the gospel according to the power of God" (2 Timothy 1:8).*

It was Paul who affirmed that we have a power working in us to do and be what God desires: *"Now to Him who is able to do exceedingly abundantly above all that we ask or think, according to the power that works in us" (Ephesians 3:20).*

In our commission to share the Gospel (Mark 16:15,16), we have been given power (Romans 1:14-16). In our need to be faithful and perservere we have been given the powerful word of God (cf. Hebrews 4:12). This is why we are able *"to be strong in the power of His might" (Ephesians 6:10).*

My cup is filled with power to do and be what God desires.

How does overflowing power impact your daily life?:

1)._____

_____

_____

_____

2)._____

_____

_____

_____

MY CUP OVERFLOWS WITH MOTIVATION

Motivation! Few things are more desirable than motivation in self and others, but it a very elusive commodity. Millions, maybe even billions, are spent annually trying to motivate people. Most seminars and workshops are no more than pep rallies; once the show is over it's back to normal. The reasons is that the only person who can motivate me for the long haul is ME. I am my own motivation expert.

Motivation is that special buzz we have in our nervous system that arouses us to take action to move toward something we want or need. No two persons are motivated the same way. In order for my cup to over flow with motivation; I must discover and apply the things that keep me motivated.

The serious Christian is ahead of the crowd relative to internal motivating factors. The best way for a Christian to stay motivated is to think on the blessings God is pouring into his cup.

What could be more motivational that the realization that we possess *"ALL spiritual blessings in Christ"*? *(Ephesians 1:3-7).* Add to this the promise of being able *"to do all* things through Christ" (Philippians 4:13). How about "For me to live is Christ, and to die is gain" (Philippians 1:22). Then there is the promise of a home in heaven (John 14:1-6; 1 Peter 1:5-7). On and on the motivation factors emerge.

In order for my cup to over flow with motivation, it will require more that simply wanting. We must prepare our hearts and attitude to do those things that create motivation. We must be "doers of the word" (James 1:23-26). God keeps on pouring.

What are some ways you keep your motivation strong and active?:

1)._____

_____

2)._____

_____

3)._____

_____

MY CUP OVERFLOWS WITH FRUIT

When I was a boy, one summer I got a job picking peaches. I loved it. One reason was because we could eat any peach that had fallen on the ground. However, it didn't take me long to lose my appetite for peaches. But today I still like peaches.

One of the rules for picking peaches was not to put too many in a basket because it would bruise the others and cause them to start rotting early. We would not let the basket "overflow" with peaches (i.e. fruit).

This isn't true relative to our spiritual cup. It is okay to let it overflow with the fruit of the Spirit. Jesus affimed that we would be known by our fruit: *"By their fruit you shall know them."* This is why we must bring forth fruit that documents our repentance.

The apostle Paul writes clearly about the fruit of the Spirit that we must produce in our daily spiritual walks. In fact, he contrasts the fruit of the Spirit with the fruit of the flesh in Galatians 5:16-26.

Here is Paul's fruit of the Spirit list; the fruit that is overflowing my cup:

> *But the fruit of the Spirit is love, joy*

peace, longsuffering, kindness, goodness,

faithfulness, gentleness, self-control.

Against such there is no law. And those

who are Christ's have crucified the flesh

with its passions and desires. If we live

in the Spirit, let us also walk in the Spirit

(Galatians 5:22-25).

Through the work of the Holy Spirit in my life, being led by God's word, I am able to not only to produce the fruit of the Spirit, but have it in an abundance so that it over flows my cup of blessings.

By the fruit of the Spirit in my life I am a positive influence on others. They are able to know that I am different from the fruit of the world (cf. 1 John 5:19).

In the Greek "Fruit of the Spirit" is one fruit, but it has the numerous facets that are mentioned. All may be produced at once in our lives.

What are some ways the fruit of the Spirit is revealed in your life?

_____

_____

_____

_____

_____

How are some ways the fruit of the flesh harm the fruit of the Spirit?

_____

_____

_____

_____

_____

MY CUP OVERFLOWS WITH CHOICES

A small boy walked back and forth in front a candy counter with a dollar in his hand. When the cleark asked him, "May I help you?" He replied, "All these choices but all I have is a dollar bill."

One of the amazing blessings that overflows my cup, is the choices I have every day. Sometimes there are so many that I find frustration creeping into my thinking.

Can you imagine a life without choices? What if we had no color choices? How would we like to have no choices relative to the clothing we wear? How about no choices relative to where we live? Yes, life is exciting, interesting, and challenging because of choices.

God creates us with the *Freedom of Choice.* He placed Adam and Eve in Paradise with the ability to make choices. Sadly, our greatest grandparents made the wrong choice. The world hasn't been the same since, as we, their descendents, have continued to make the wrong choices.

Joshua reminds us of the seriousness of choices: *"Choose you this day whom you will serve, as for me and my house we will serve the Lord" (Joshua 24:15).* Therefore, in making the right choices, I ask God for wisdom to do so properly and in harmony with His will (cf. James 1:1-6).

My cup over-flows with choices of friends, associates, behavior, attitudes, how I will serve others, and what I choose to read and apply to my life. I choose God's word. I choose to worship Him *"in spirit and in truth" (John 4:23, 24)*.

I have the power to choose the paths I will walk today; the power to serve others and bring blessings into their lives. My cup is overflowing with choices.

My desire is to make all of my choices based on God's will and word. This isn't easy. Why? Sometimes I'm not sure, so this is when I study the word closer and pray with more diligence.

What are the pluses and minuses of having so many choices?

_____

_____

_____

_____

Why did God create us with Freedom of Choice?

_____

_____

_____

_____

What is the most difficult choice you have had to make?

_____

_____

_____

_____

MY CUP OVERFLOWS WITH INSPIRATION

Mary rolls out of bed, not with her usual reluctance, but with an amazing burst of energy. In the kitchen she, as the old rock and roll song says, "rattles those pots and pans."

A bit annoyed, her husband asks her what in the world is she up to so early in the morning? Mary replies with a smile, "Oh, I just, for some reason, felt inspired to try a new receipt that I read about last night."

Inspiration! We've all had those moments of inspiration. As a child of the King, my cup continually overflows with inspiration. Webster defines _inspiration_ as "*an inspiring influence; and stimulus to creative thought or action ... an inspired idea, action ... influenced upon a human being.*"

God has provided so many things that inspire me. It all starts with His unqualified loved for me (cf. John 3:16). When I gaze into the heavens, I am awed by the majesty of His creation. The laughter of a child, the chirping of a bird, the howl of the wolf.

Jesus taught that the cure for worry was taking time to consider the wonders around us. "*So why do you worry about clothing? Consider the lilies of the field, how they* grow: *they neither toil nor spin; and yet I say to you that even Solomon in all his glory was not arrayed like one of these"* (Matthew 6:28, 29).

It is obvious that I am inspired by the *"inspired word of God."* Paul wrote very clearly about the amazing power of God's word in our lives (cf. 2 Timothy 3:15-17).

My cup overflows with inspiration when I think about how, that in Christ, *"I am not condemned"* (cf. Romans 8:1, 2), and am the receipient of *"All spiritual blessings in Christ* (cf. Ephesians 1:3-7).

With all the inspiration provided by God, I have never understood why some of His children aren't motivated. Sadly, they act like their walk with God is a real burden, not a journey of joy and wonder.

We need to read Isaiah 6:1-6 over and over. We need to have the "vision" the prophet had of our awesome and all-powerful Father in heaven. When we do there will be no stopping of the overflowing inspiration to be and do what God desires.

What are some additional things that should cause our cup to overflow with inspiration?

_____

_____

_____

What is your greatest inspiration? Why?

_____

_____

_____

_____

_____

MAINTANENCE OF MY CUP

Few things are more repulsive to a housewife than a sink full of dirty dishes. If we are served a cup of coffee in a restraurant we quickly examine it to see if it is clean; lipstick marks are dead giveaways that the cup hasn't been washed properly.

As a Christian I must keep my cup washed and clean: inside and out. Here is how Jesus put it to the scribes and Pharisees: *"Woe to you, scribes and Pharisees, hypocrites! For you cleanse the outside the cup and dish, but inside they are full of extortion and self-indulgence. Blind Pharisees, first cleanse the inside of the cup and dish, that the outside of them may be clean also" (Matthew 23:25, 26).*

The maintanence of my spiritual cup involves my thinking, attitude, beliefs, and feelings. It is facilitated by *"setting my mind on things above" (Colosians 3:2).* It is directed by following the thinking agenda Paul gave us in *Philippians 4:6-10.*

A clean cup is an overflowing cup. A cup contaminated by unwholesome thoughts and attitudes will not overflow. It will be flled with debree placed there by Satan via all his tools and tactics. This is why we must *"Resist the Devils so he will flee from us."*

Through planned prayer, Bible study, worship, and meditation on God's word, we are able to keep our cups clean. A clean cup guarantees an overflowing cup. We need to wash the inside with praise and honor given to God, remembering He is the one pouring the overflowing blessings into our cups.

What is your plan and practice for keeping your cup clean and functional?:

1)._____

_____

_____

_____

THE AUTHOR

Made in the USA
Charleston, SC
09 March 2015